# Motivating Staff

**Chrissie Wright**

# DIRECTORY OF SOCIAL CHANGE

Published by
Directory of Social Change
24 Stephenson Way
London NW1 2DP
Tel. 08450 77 77 07; Fax 020 7391 4804
email publications@dsc.org.uk
www.dsc.org.uk
from whom further copies and a full books catalogue are available.

Directory of Social Change is a Registered Charity no. 800517

First published 2010

ISBN 978 1 906294 14 4

British Library Cataloguing in Publication Data

A catalogue record for this book is available from the British Library

Cover and text designed by Kate Bass
Typeset by Marlinzo Services, Frome
Printed and bound by Martins the Printers, Berwick-upon-Tweed

All Directory of Social Change departments in London:
08450 77 77 07

Directory of Social Change Northern Office:
Research 0151 708 0136

For other titles in the DSC SPEED READ series go to:
www.dsc.org.uk/Publications/SpeedReadSeries

# Contents

Introduction    **4**

**Chapter 1: The basics**    **5**
- What is motivation?    5
- Why should you motivate people?    5
- Who is responsible for motivating people at work?    6

**Chapter 2: Communication**    **7**
- Listening    7
- Walking the job    9
- One-to-one meetings    10
- Appraisals    11
- Staff forums    11
- Observation and conversations    12
- Exercises    13

**Chapter 3: Basic needs at work**    **14**
- Physical environment, safety and security    14
- Social environment    15
- Confidence and self-esteem    15

**Chapter 4: Learning and development**    **18**
- Creating a culture of learning and development    18
- Setting objectives    20
- Offering challenges    20
- Coaching and mentoring    21
- The benefits    23

**Chapter 5: Managing people's well-being**    **24**
- Changes or problems at work    24
- Changes or problems at home    25
- When all is well    28

**Chapter 6: Your beliefs: a help or a hindrance?**    **29**
- Douglas McGregor's Theory X and Theory Y    29
- Believing in people's potential    31

# Introduction

## Who is this book for?

This practical guide will help managers who are responsible for the performance of others. In particular, it will support individuals who are new to management and add value to more experienced managers.

## What will it give you?

This book demonstrates that you can help to motivate people and that the skills to create the right conditions for this to happen can be learned. It teaches you how to get the best out of your staff, emphasising communication, good processes, a culture of learning and development and a belief in people as the keys to effective motivation. In addition, it will help you to deal with obstacles to active motivation, whether they arise from work or home.

# Chapter 1

# The basics

*This chapter covers the what and why of motivation and who is responsible for motivating staff.*

## What is motivation?

Motivation is what makes people do things: it is what makes them put real effort and energy into what they do. So, to motivate people means to give them a cause to do something. It also means to encourage the interest of a person, and stems from the Latin *movere*, 'to move'.

## Why should you motivate people?

Not everybody believes that you should invest time in motivating people or that you *can*. Some people may think that there are those who are naturally lazy and don't want to work, and that the only way to get these people to do what needs to be done is the threat of a reprimand for not getting a job done (see more on this on p. 30).

The premise of this book is that there *are* things that you can do to create an environment that will allow the vast majority of people to become self-motivated and interested in their work. Further, the benefit of making these changes is that people can perform better, will achieve a lot more and are happier when they are motivated.

**Case study**

Julian did his job with a sense of keenness and always wanting to do well. However, after a couple of years his manager left and a new manager started. She didn't communicate with him well and tried to micro-manage his workload, despite his proven track record. He became apathetic and cynical and the problem was never addressed. Eventually, he left the organisation.

## Top tip

It is not the job of the human resources (HR) function to motivate staff. HR can advise and guide line managers about best motivational practice, but it is the line manager's job to create the right climate for motivation in their teams.

**Heather Brierley, Training Consultant, DSC**

# Who is responsible for motivating people at work?

People often believe that motivation comes from within, and while this is true to some extent, external factors and conditions can deeply affect people's levels of motivation. Consider the following two things:

1  the word demotivate
2  creating a motivating environment.

First, demotivate: this means 'make less likely to work or make an effort', which implies that if someone is demotivated the trigger is external. If someone in your team shows a sudden change of behavior and signs of demotivation then, as their manager, it is your responsibility to try and find the cause and, if possible, to work with the team member to resolve the situation. The causes may be many and complex, including the current management style and approach.

Second, a motivating environment. Motivating people is not about doing anything to people; it is about creating the right environment that allows people to give their best: one in which people feel valued and freed up to use their knowledge and skills and to develop their creative abilities in a purposeful way, with a clear sense of why and what they are doing.

Creating this motivating environment is your responsibility, and also the responsibility of everyone in the organisation.

# Chapter 2

# Communication

*This chapter covers listening, walking the job, one-to-ones, appraisals, staff forums, observation and conversation, and exercises.*

Good communication is the bedrock of good motivation: you cannot motivate people without communicating with them well.

## Listening

Think about how good you are at listening.

*Checklist*

- ❑ My mind sometimes wanders when I am listening to others.
- ❑ I mentally prepare the point I am going to make before the other person has finished speaking.
- ❑ Sometimes I assume that I know the point that the person is going to make (although I may be wrong).
- ❑ If I agree with the points that a person is making, I get animated and want to interrupt with my thoughts on the subject.
- ❑ Sometimes I get frustrated waiting for people to get to the point.
- ❑ If I have other things on my mind, I can end up thinking about something completely different, then 'zone into' the conversation having missed part of what the other person is saying.

> **Top tip**
>
> I believe listening is an attitude, not a skill: when you genuinely want to hear what someone has to say, you will pay close attention and listen carefully. If you want to be an effective listener, then the trick is to make yourself want to hear.
>
> **Debra Allcock Tyler, Chief Executive, DSC**

❑ During telephone meetings with colleagues, sometimes I do other tasks on my computer and miss the points being made.

Most of us would recognise that we do one or more of these things on a regular basis. So how can we improve? It is tricky to get other people to change how they listen, so it is best to think about how to improve your own listening skills and to take into account that the people you are managing may not be hanging on your every word, particularly in group briefings or meetings.

## Your listening skills

Simply by being more self-aware and honest with yourself about how good a listener you are can help you to improve your listening skills: use the listening checklist to help you identify some of the things you do that you should stop doing. The next time you find yourself doing one of these things you will be more likely to check yourself and stop a potentially wandering mind in its tracks.

Sometimes it may be hard to concentrate if someone you are managing has trouble getting to the point or is not a great communicator. In these cases you just need to have patience and to avoid the temptation of telling them what you think they are thinking. Instead, ask questions to help guide them towards clarifying what they are saying.

## Improving how others listen to you

You can minimise the risk that people will 'zone out' from what you are saying by keeping to the point, summarising the key points you are making, and asking specific questions to check that the information has been taken in.

In addition, you should think about how you communicate with regard to your tone of voice and body language, and what might distract people from listening. For example, if you sound negative or bored about a new project, it is unlikely that the people listening are going to be particularly excited about it.

If you are standing in front of your team members, think about your posture – stand confidently. Watch out for any distracting habits you may have: possibly verbal 'ticks' such as repeatedly saying the same word ('like' or 'kind of' are common), or physical ones such as clicking your pen or putting your hair behind your ears.

## Walking the job

Walking the job is the practice of getting out of your office or from behind your desk to talk, listen and show an interest in the people with whom you work. Hearts and minds can only be won face-to-face: you cannot hope to motivate your staff effectively from behind a computer screen. The concept of walking the job applies to anyone in a management position. The more senior your position, the greater the proportion of your time should be spent walking the job (because you have more people to communicate with).

### Why should you walk the job?

Many managers feel uncomfortable at the idea of walking about, believing that they should be doing something more useful. If you feel this way, try to ignore it. Walking the job has the enormous benefit of motivating staff because those in charge show that they are interested in the people doing the work. It results in direct feedback, increased understanding and faster problem-solving.

**Top tip**

Don't worry about having something specific to discuss before walking the job. The aim is to encourage staff to be open with you: the less it feels like there is a strict agenda, the more people will feel encouraged to be open and bring up things that they wish to discuss.

**Top tip**

When you walk the job, make sure that you say how important having the chance to talk with them is to you, and thank them for taking the time.

## Top tip

If you are a senior manager and speaking to those you don't manage directly, explain that you will be discussing the suggestions with other line managers concerned, and that those managers will be communicating any responses. Doing this keeps line managers informed and ensures that they don't feel left out or undermined.

## Dos and don'ts

**Do** schedule a regular time in your diary, perhaps once a fortnight or month, to walk the job. Be realistic about how much time you can make available, and be ruthless about protecting it.

**Don't** just go to places where you get a good reception or (if you are a senior manager) leave out any smaller departments.

**Do** vary your route and your timing.

**Don't** stand on ceremony. Sit down to talk to individuals or small groups.

**Do** be honest about why you are there. 'I just wanted to hear about how things are going', 'I heard some good news about the grant, so I'd thought I'd come along to hear about it personally.'

**Don't** do too much talking: look, question and listen as people talk about their job and their concerns. Usually they will be delighted to explain what is going on.

**Do** gather suggestions as you go.

## One-to-one meetings

It is really good practice and very important to have regular one-to-one meetings (one-to-ones) at least once a month with each of the people who you manage. If your organisation does not have this policy, or if you don't have many one-to-ones, you should initiate them with your team members (and recommend having them across the organisation), or start having them more often.

While walking the job is a very useful thing to do, one-to-ones offer you an opportunity to get to the nub of any issues, and your team members can talk freely about whatever concerns them without anyone else around. For example, if someone has a personal issue or a problem with a team mate, they are not going to feel comfortable discussing it in a group. One-to-ones also give you time to review the progress that has been made following any targets that you and your team members have set.

Never cancel a one-to-one: doing so sends a message that something is more important than your member of staff. Of course in reality there will be times when you have to postpone a one-to-one. There are two things you can do to make sure this happens properly: 1) explain the reasons why you cannot make the meeting and 2) rearrange the meeting immediately to demonstrate that it is important to you and is not an optional event.

## Appraisals

If your organisation does not have a formal appraisal process or performance review, you should definitely establish one and try to influence to get it in place across the board.

It is an important process that allows members of staff to highlight the areas in which they are doing well and those in which they feel they can develop. Following this, together with your team, you can set targets for training and development for the next year. It creates time for you and your team members to reflect on how well you are working with each of them and gives you a chance to learn from the past.

## Staff forums

While walking the job, one-to-ones and appraisals will go a long way to ensuring that you have effective communication, there still may be areas in which your team members might hold back. It is quite natural to want to present the best side of yourself to your

**Top tip**

There are three main things you should consider in appraisals:
(1) make sure you prepare and encourage preparation from the appraisee;
(2) involve appraisees: an appraisal isn't *done* to someone: it should be a two-way process;
(3) keep the focus on the positive and the future as far as possible, although poor performance may need to be addressed.

**Cathy Shimmin, Senior Training Manager, DSC**

**Where next?**

Look up 'appraisals' under the alphabetical index at: www.business balls.com

## Top tip

A staff forum must be managed well by forum leaders to ensure that meetings are not a 'whinge session' or a space to raise personal grievances about line managers. In the first meeting, the chair and forum members should set ground rules together to make sure everyone has ownership of them.

manager, and so it is probable that there will be situations in which your team members don't feel that they can be fully honest with you.

A way around this is to start a staff forum. A staff forum can help to you to get more honest and direct feedback, and can be motivating for staff as it helps them to have more of an involvement in the wider organisation.

Staff and managers would need to buy into the idea fully (recognising that they would need to provide any cover necessary while they have the meetings), and you need to have staff members who are willing to take on the responsibility of organising, chairing and minuting the meetings. Also, someone from the management team (preferably the chief executive or equivalent) will need to make themselves available to staff forum leaders in order to hear feedback.

A staff forum can be a lot of work, but don't let this put you off: the benefits outweigh the costs. However, make sure you consider how much work it will involve so that you can be realistic about how much time and effort it will take.

## Observation and conversations

An obvious fact is that everyone is different. While there will be some common things that most people are motivated by, such as the need for achievement and recognition, beyond that each person will be motivated by different things. Communication is the key to finding out what these different motivations are. At the basic level you need to get to know the people you manage and make observations (but not assumptions) through your daily interactions. During conversations you can find out more about their motivations simply by asking 'What do you think motivates you?' or 'What do you enjoy doing the most?' and 'What do you enjoy doing the least?'

## Exercises

It can be a huge benefit to do a range of communication exercises with your team. These exercises can help all of us to understand why we behave in the way we do, and highlight the areas in which we can develop.

The important thing to consider before doing any sort of team exercise is *why* you are doing it. Is the climate right? For example, if there is a lot of hostility in the team or someone who is really dominant within it, you may need to deal with this in other ways such as in one-to-ones.

In addition, you need to consider your level of knowledge and experience of communication or personality styles exercises before you decide to do one with your team. You must understand how they work and be careful to explain what the aim of doing them is and their advantages and limits. If they are not handled properly, some people may find them limiting and simplistic or even threatening.

If you don't have any experience of doing these sorts of exercises or the psychological theories that underpin them, it would be better to find someone who is experienced and who could run an exercise for you and your team. Indeed, if you have the resources, you could do a formal paid training day with a qualified practitioner or facilitator who runs one of the many options out there such as the Myers-Briggs Type Indicator® assessment, FIRO-B® or Strength Deployment Inventory®. Otherwise you could find someone within your organisation who does have experience or make contact with someone who would be willing to do it for free, or for an exchange of resources.

**Where next?**

See the 'communication style test' on pp. 34–39 in *The Pleasure and the Pain: The No-fibbing Guide to Working with People*, **D Allcock Tyler, DSC, 2007.**

# Chapter 3

# Basic needs at work

*This chapter covers the foundations that people need at work before they can be actively motivated, and shows you how to ensure your team members feel valued.*

## Physical environment, safety and security

It is obviously important that your team members have a suitable work environment and feel safe and secure at work. Without these things in place they are likely to be uncomfortable or distracted and will not be able to concentrate on doing their jobs well. These include:

- being paid on time and in full
- having health and safety requirements met
- holiday pay
- adequate maternity and paternity leave and pay
- allowance for time off regarding personal or family members' health
- pension services
- a grievance procedure
- job security.

Managers have some accountability to ensure that these obligations are met, but the overall responsibility is with the HR department or the equivalent person or people who deal with these matters in your organisation.

You can have some impact in this area: for example, you can make sure that your team members are aware of the organisation's policies and procedures and that you are sensible with regard to them taking off a reasonable amount of time when they need to for health and other reasons.

## Social environment

There are basic things that you can do to make people feel valued and to create an inclusive feeling and social belonging in your team.

*Checklist*

- ❑ Regularly walk the job, have one-to-ones (see pp. 9–10) and take an interest in what is happening.
- ❑ Share an interest in employees' lives and what they hold to be important.
- ❑ Create an atmosphere of teamwork and friendliness. This can be as simple as offering to make everyone cups of tea or initiating friendly conversation, or remembering to buy a cake and a card for team members' birthdays.
- ❑ Make new team members feel welcome: take them out for lunch and show them the local area, for example.

Of course, you can only go so far to create an inclusive atmosphere: you cannot *make* a new member of the team fit into social groups at work, for example.

## Confidence and self-esteem

You can have a significant impact on the self-esteem of your team members at work. If you can tick off all of the items in the following list, you are likely to have team members who feel valued, who understand the

**Where next?**

*Team Building,* B Rothwell, DSC, 2009.

**Top tip**

Be sensitive with negative feedback: never chastise someone in public and (unless it is regarding a misdemeanour) present it as an opportunity for improvement rather than a reprimand. Well-handled negative feedback can be a motivator.

## Case study

The Directory of Social Change holds monthly staff briefings where each manager briefs the people in their teams about the organisation's activities and financial figures for the last month. Managers also use briefing as an opportunity to announce the particular achievements of teams, people or the organisation, and to discuss things of importance to the whole organisation such as the vision, mission and objectives.

importance of what your organisation does, and who know their place and significance within it.

### Checklist

- ❑ Recognise team members privately and publicly.
- ❑ Report regularly on the team's progress to the team and the wider organisation.
- ❑ Appraise the performance of all team members (see p. 11).
- ❑ Make sure that all of your team know the importance of their contribution to the organisation.
- ❑ Ensure that every member knows and understands the organisation's vision, mission and objectives, and why the work being done matters.
- ❑ Explain the organisation's results and achievements regularly to your team members.

### Recognition

What is the best way to recognise staff members? Although generally speaking the best way to acknowledge someone is face-to-face, you should consider the different ways in which people like to receive praise. Some people may find it embarrassing to be acknowledged verbally in front of others: they may appreciate it much more to receive a handwritten card or note. Some might prefer to be recognised during one-to-ones. Others may like to have their achievements trumpeted across the organisation.

You will find out the best ways to recognise your team members once you know them and understand their preferences.

### Dos and don'ts

**Do** be specific with praise. Rather than saying 'You're doing a good job', say for example, 'Thanks James, you did a great job writing that report. It was really well

*Checklist*

- ❑ Set and clearly communicate objectives that will stretch either individuals or the team.
- ❑ Provide the scope for every individual to take on more responsibility.
- ❑ Promote creativity and new ideas.
- ❑ Encourage staff to implement their own initiatives.

As with setting goals, you will need to consider the level of experience of your team members before considering what might challenge them. People need different levels and types of intervention and support at different stages in their jobs. A new employee will find simply getting to know the job challenging, while a more experienced team member might not need supervisory support but would need other types such as coaching.

## Coaching and mentoring

As a part of your job as a manager you can have different sorts of conversations with the people who you manage, and these can come from a management, coaching or mentoring angle. On the one hand, integrating the techniques of coaching and mentoring into your day-to-day management is important. On the other hand, it might be useful to have people outside your team who are designated coaches or mentors to individuals in your team. If you try being a full mentor or coach for one or more of your team members, you may end up spending too much time with one or two people at the expense of others. If you manage one person it may be more realistic, but an outside person still may be more suitable with regard to experience.

In many ways coaching and mentoring are very similar. They are about the development and growth of people and their abilities at work, asking questions

**Top tip**

'Management conversations are all about the *what* of the individual's level of performance, as judged by the standards set by the organisation . . . Coaching conversations are all about enhancing the individual's awareness of *how* they can achieve optimum performance.'

**Sheridan Maguire,** *Core Coaching*, DSC, 2008, pp. 2–3

**Where next?**

**How to Improve Performance through Coaching,** DSC course, www.dsc.org.uk/ Training/ Management andgovernance

21

and listening, and building a relationship with the person. They are also about challenging people.

Where the two differ is that coaching is about increasing levels of performance using specific goals. It is concerned more with the short-term and urgency, but also can help with longer-term goals. Mentoring is about longer-term career development and sharing knowledge. In this way, mentors are chosen for their expertise, experience and knowledge: the role can be more advisory and a bit less questioning. Coaches don't necessarily need to be experienced in this way, but do need to know the techniques for the right conversations with people in order to help them unlock their potential and achieve results.

### Manager-as-coach

A book of this size cannot go into all the ins and outs of coaching. If you are not familiar with coaching at work, you should think about integrating it into your day-to-day management and looking into it further (look at the 'Where nexts' on pp. 21 and 23 to see where to find out more).

In a nutshell, coaching conversations:

- must focus on achieving a specific result
- need to be structured and have purpose and direction, but should not be rigid
- are driven by the person being coached, not the coach
- should uncover the person's understanding of an issue, which will allow them to work out for themselves the actions that need to be taken
- should ask probing but non-leading questions, in order to help the person to work things out for themselves by looking at an issue from a different perspective.

**Top tip**

'Buddying' staff – especially during their induction or in secondments – can be a great way to impart learning. It is mutually beneficial, providing 'newbies' with support and a sense of belonging, and allowing the more experienced to lead through knowledge sharing and supporting others' development.

**Cathy Shimmin, Senior Training Manager, DSC**

## The benefits

If your staff members can fulfil their potential at work it means that, beyond the initial target-setting that you provide, they are taking responsibility for most of their own workloads and actions. The ultimate accountability as manager still rests with you, but depending on their varying levels of experience, each team member is working more or less independently, with you conducting spot checks every now and again to make sure that everything is working as it should be.

In this situation, not only do you have more time to manage people properly, rather than supervising or micro-managing, but members of staff feel more motivated by being more self-directed.

**Where next?**

*Core Coaching,* S Maguire, DSC, 2008.

# Chapter 5

# Managing people's well-being

*This chapter addresses the issues that can interfere with motivating people and shows you how to deal with them.*

## Changes or problems at work

When individuals are suddenly hit by something that makes them feel insecure, this will dominate their thoughts and interfere in their performance at work. These setbacks can happen in situations such as the example in the case study, or in instances of bullying and harassment.

Changes and new things at work such as an organisational restructure can also have an impact. While this can be exciting it can also cause insecurity and leave people with lots of questions which will occupy their minds, such as 'What will it be like working with these new people?' and 'How will it impact on me on a daily basis?' Allow them to discuss their concerns and go through the practical implications for them – is there any extra support they will need during the transition?

The reality is that we all have our ups and downs, and when you are affected by a problem or a change, you try to minimise the impact it has on your work and on others (possibly with the help of your manager). Similarly, when it happens to the people you manage, you can help them to minimise the impact it has on their work and on others.

If you handle these sorts of circumstances badly, it can cause people to feel insecure, which will be actively demotivating. With this in mind, the most important things you should do are to:

- make sure that you're available to people: be approachable
- communicate regularly with your team members
- treat people like adults
- model positive behaviours.

You can consider the potential negative impacts of any given difficult situation and put plans into place to minimise the impact when problems arise. Again, ensure that your organisation has the proper policies and procedures and that your team members can access them: in a staff handbook, for example.

## Changes or problems at home

You can put plans into place for what to do about issues arising at work, but what about problems at home spilling over into work? A person you are managing may be going through a difficult time: perhaps relationship trouble or difficulty sleeping; their child might be having issues at school or their partner may be very sick. Although these are private matters, if the individual's concentration at work has diminished or they are taking an increasing number of days off to deal with the problem, this can become a problem at work. The most important thing is not to ignore the issue.

> **Top tip**
>
> **If you are resistant to being flexible when dealing with shorter-term problems you can risk intensifying the problem. At this level, it is likely that the person involved will be able to make up any missed time at a later point.**
>
> **Jill Thornton, Personnel Co-ordinator, DSC**

You can go through a series of steps to help someone in this situation.

1 Arrange a one-to-one meeting.

2 Acknowledge that you have noticed they are struggling and ask what the issue is: the first thing is for them to acknowledge that there is a problem.

3 Ask them if there is anything that you or anyone else could do to help them, including support with their workload.

4 If they decline the offer of help, you can still suggest some practical steps to take such as taking regular breaks, talking with colleagues or talking with an appropriate professional for support. If you need to, speak to your HR manager if you have one or your line manager for guidance regarding more serious or potentially long-term problems.

5 For shorter-term problems such as moving house or ongoing but not serious medical conditions, you can agree to a level of flexibility with regard to working hours to help get them through it.

6 For serious or potentially long-term problems, you may need to draw up a plan or timescale for long-term management of the situation.

### Mid-level, serious or potentially long-term problems

Obviously, more serious medical conditions, difficulties in relationships with partners or children or a partner being out of work will be more problematic and stressful. In these situations you may need to give some compassionate leave. Often this will come down to a two-way trust issue: you need to balance their needs against those of the team and organisation.

You can suggest that at some point the time will be made up, although this may not always be possible, especially with part-time workers. At this point you are trying to manage a mid-level problem so that it does

**Top tip**

Think about the language you use. If you frame the situation as a problem they will become defensive. Instead, try to see, and help others to see, possibilities and solutions rather than limits and problems. Present it as an opportunity to solve something together.

**Cathy Shimmin, Senior Training Manager, DSC**

not escalate into a serious long-term issue. Again, if this means giving some time to avoid an escalation of the problem, then this is an investment rather than a cost.

There are, of course, many possible reasons for long-term problems. Depression, for example, is a common difficulty that many people come up against in their lives, and must be dealt with properly and sensitively in the workplace.

## Case study

A manager at a medium-sized charity began to present symptoms of depression: he was finding it difficult to cope with his workload, was disengaged in meetings and became very irritable in situations when normally he would be fine.

On noticing these symptoms, his manager arranged a one-to-one meeting. They sat down and she asked him to explain what had been happening. He said that he was going through a period of depression: he knew that this was the case as it had happened before. It also transpired that he was not receiving any treatment at that time.

He was advised to seek help from his doctor and that if he needed it, support would be offered at work. The doctor advised three weeks' sick leave and medication, which he took. Nothing was heard from him in this time, so the HR manager contacted him. He said that he needed a couple more weeks, and sent in another doctor's certificate.

He was supported in taking time, and during the two weeks the manager and the HR manager arranged a home visit to see how he was and to get a picture of where he was in the recovery process. He was getting better, and they sat down to make a plan of how he could be supported in his return to work. They offered him flexi-hours or part-time work for a further two weeks to help him get back into the swing of things, which he took.
He returned to work feeling fully supported and understood, and was able to resume all his work activities.

In any situation when someone needs to take time off, you should ensure that you brief the other people in your team, and in the wider organisation if necessary, on what is happening. Obviously you will need to find a way to communicate it without breaching confidentiality, and you should agree what will be said with the person concerned. In addition, you should make sure that their workload is not completely dropped in their absence.

Again, you should ensure that your organisation has the appropriate policies and procedures in place to deal with these sorts of situations. This will include policies or procedures for compassionate leave, flexible working, homeworking and sickness.

## When all is well

It is also important to maintain people's well-being during times when there are no great changes or problems. It sends a message to staff that their health and well-being is important to you, which is a motivator in itself.

Here are some examples of what your organisation can do:

- Promote healthier journeys to work by taking advantage of the government's Cycle to Work scheme which 'allows employers to loan cycles and cyclist's safety equipment to employees as a tax-free benefit' (see tinyurl.com/cycle2workguide).
- Cover some of the costs for eye care such as for eye tests and possibly a contribution towards the cost of the glasses.
- Encourage people to set up lunchtime runs around the park or similar activities – this can help physical well-being but also promote social interaction.
- Encourage people to take short breaks away from the computer to rest their eyes, and to take their lunch breaks.
- Promote a work–life balance by modelling this through your own behaviour.

**Top tip**

Take care not to shift the problem onto your shoulders entirely: the person concerned needs to take responsibility and acknowledge that there is something to overcome.

**Top tip**

Start having welcome parties as well as leaving dos. It makes new people feel valued and is a positive thing to do, no matter whether times are good or bad.

**Jill Thornton, Personnel Co-ordinator, DSC**

# Chapter 6

# Your beliefs: a help or a hindrance?

*This final chapter looks at the different beliefs that managers may have about the people who they manage and the importance of believing in people's potential.*

## Douglas McGregor's Theory X and Theory Y

In his 1960 book *The Human Side of Enterprise*, McGregor put forward the idea that a manager's interactions with employees would be largely determined by the manager's own beliefs. A manager's belief system about people's motivation may lean towards one of his theories: Theory X or Theory Y.

**Theory X managers believe that people:**

- dislike work and will avoid it if at all possible

- must be forced or bribed to put in the right amount of effort to achieve objectives

- prefer to be directed than accept responsibilities

- are motivated mainly by anxiety about their security and do not have much ambition

**Theory Y managers believe that people:**

- do not have an inborn dislike of work and will work willingly when it is a source of fulfilment

- impose discipline on themselves when they are committed to a goal, and will do so because of associated rewards with regard to satisfaction and self-fulfilment

- will not only accept responsibility but look for it

- usually have the potential for a high amount of creativity and inventiveness at work

**Top tip**

Knowing that your manager believes in you and is fully supporting you (rather than looking over your shoulder to see what you have done wrong) is vitally important in order to build a relationship built on respect and trust.

## *Theory X managers*

We can conclude from these points that managers who mostly support Theory X will tend to be controlling, make decisions on behalf of others, closely monitor them and force through change.

## *Theory Y managers*

Theory Y managers are likely to allow people to have more self-direction in their work, to manage their own workloads and set goals collaboratively. They may be more encouraging of new ideas and expect their team members to take responsibility for themselves and their self-development at work.

## A bit of both

In reality, managers are likely to think different things about people on different days. Some managers may think that certain individuals in their team are just not interested and don't want to take responsibility, while others are involved and actively seek responsibility. Perhaps you find yourself thinking 'He's just not interested – he doesn't want to know'. If this is the case, this should be your trigger to start reconsidering your way of thinking.

## Believing in people's potential

You can try going through all the motions and ticking off all the boxes, but still end up being a Theory X manager at times. When you find yourself thinking that someone just isn't interested, first ask yourself a few questions. Are you being fair? Are you being open? Are you motivating your staff by modelling the behaviour that you want to see? Also, how many people really do lack motivation completely?

You can take practical steps to change your mindset. One way would be to find out what interests your team members outside work. If you see that someone who seems apathetic in the workplace is dynamic and motivated in another sphere, you will see that they do have the capacity to be motivated.

You may find that someone who seems unmotivated to you at work willingly takes on positions of responsibility outside: perhaps volunteering to run the allotment association, coaching the school football team or arranging the fair at the town hall. People often turn their excess energies and talents to what interests them, and perhaps merely tolerate their jobs as a way of earning a living. However, it does not have to continue this way: it is about providing the right environment and challenges to

**Top tip**

The simple act in itself of paying individuals attention, and asking them what interests them, can go a long way to helping people feel different about their level of motivation.

31

bring out the inner motivation in these people (see chapter 4).

These sorts of conversations can crop up when you walk the job, in one-to-one meetings or appraisals (see pp. 9–10). Once you know what motivates someone outside work, you can help set off a train of thought by asking them to think about how they see work. Encourage them to approach work with a different perspective: what is it about the things that motivate them outside that could be transferred to work? This may just be about a change of attitude, but you also may be able to take advantage of the person's skills or interests that you did not know about before.

Remember that you can only point people in the right direction and facilitate their development. Ultimately, once you have posed all the right questions, listened well and given ample opportunities for development, it is down to the individual to take it from there. If there are no improvements, it might be time to have a wider conversation about career development and the person's future direction. If the conclusion is that they are in the wrong job, you may be able to help them move to another more suitable part of the organisation if possible, or to pastures new.

Finally, remember that you are not necessarily a friend as a manager. Concentrate on being the best you can: a combination of manager, counsellor, mentor and coach, and a dependable person who your team members can trust.

**Top tip**

When you've done everything you can, don't take it personally and don't take it home.

**Cathy Shimmin, Senior Training Manager, DSC**